D0602195

SACRAMENTO PUBLIC LIBRARY
828 "I" STREET
SACRAMENTO, CA 95814
5/2011

CICADAS!
STRANGE AND WONDERFUL

LAURENCE PRINGLE
ILLUSTRATED BY MERYL HENDERSON

BOYDS MILLS PRESS

HONESDALE, PENNSYLVANIA

Cicadas may, indeed, be wondrous to behold, but even more so to Peter Jacobi is his beloved granddaughter, Chloe, to whom he dedicates this book.
—*L. P.*

In memory of Faith, who supported everything I did with love and enthusiasm. I couldn't have had a better friend.
—*M. H.*

The author wishes to thank cicada experts Dr. David C. Marshall and Kathy Hill, Department of Ecology and Evolutionary Biology, University of Connecticut, for their thorough review of the manuscript and illustrations.

Text copyright © 2010 by Laurence Pringle
Illustrations copyright © 2010 by Meryl Henderson
All rights reserved

Boyds Mills Press, Inc.
815 Church Street
Honesdale, Pennsylvania 18431
Printed in the United States of America

ISBN: 978-1-59078-673-4

Library of Congress Control Number: 2010925563

First edition
The text of this book is set in 14.5-point Clearface Regular.
The illustrations are done in watercolor.

10 9 8 7 6 5 4 3 2 1

Town Braces for Insect Invasion!
Hordes of Insects Overrun Community!
Attack of the 17-Year Locusts!

Almost every year, in parts of the United States, you may read or hear news of these unusual insects. Are they dangerous?

3

No! The insects are harmless cicadas, NOT locusts. Cicadas live on every continent except Antarctica. Their buzzing sounds are a common outdoor noise—a symbol of sunny summer days.

In North America, certain kinds of cicadas appear in huge numbers. These species live mostly in the eastern United States but can be found as far west as Nebraska, Kansas, Oklahoma, and Texas. Every thirteen or seventeen years, in different places, millions of cicadas suddenly emerge from the ground. These amazing insects are called periodical cicadas. No other insects in North America excite as much wonder and curiosity.

Cicada is pronounced sih-KAY-duh.

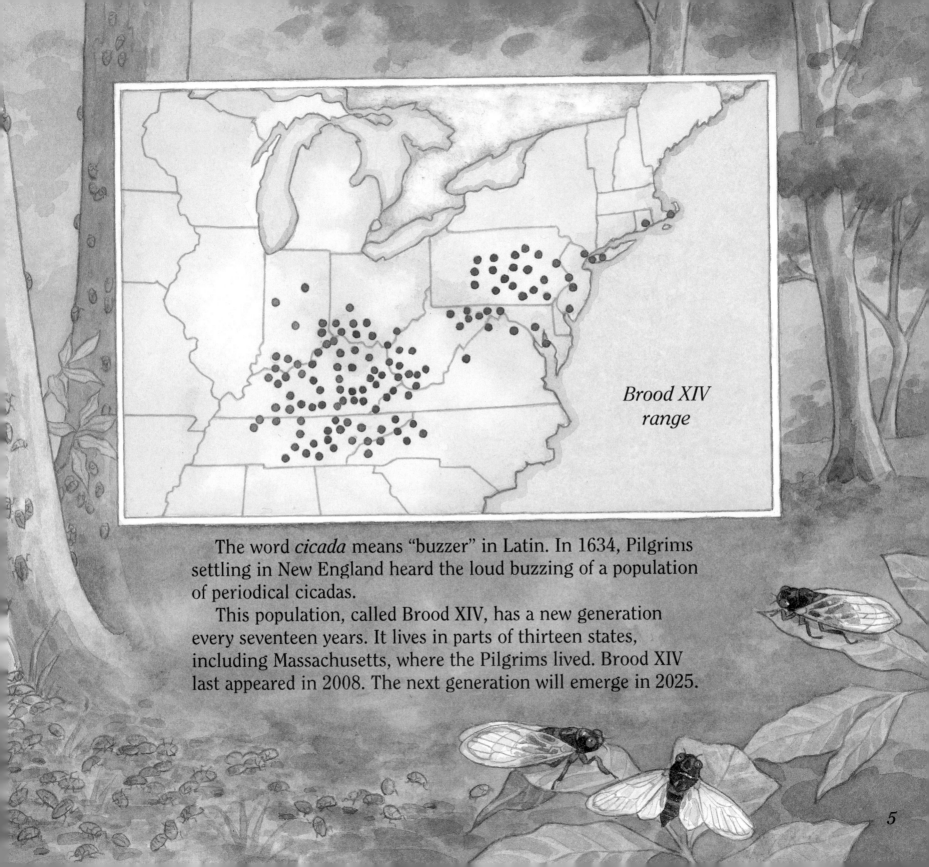

Brood XIV
range

The word *cicada* means "buzzer" in Latin. In 1634, Pilgrims
settling in New England heard the loud buzzing of a population
of periodical cicadas.

This population, called Brood XIV, has a new generation
every seventeen years. It lives in parts of thirteen states,
including Massachusetts, where the Pilgrims lived. Brood XIV
last appeared in 2008. The next generation will emerge in 2025.

The Pilgrims worried as they saw countless cicadas crawling over the ground and climbing plants. They remembered Bible stories of "plagues of locusts" that destroyed crops. So the Pilgrims were the first to mistakenly call cicadas "locusts."

Locusts are grasshoppers. They are called short-horned grasshoppers because they have a pair of short antennae on their heads. Locusts and other grasshoppers are related to crickets and katydids. All of these insects are in a group (order) called Orthoptera. And all of these insects have chewing mouthparts.

The Pilgrims had some reason to fear locusts. Throughout history, vast swarms of these grasshoppers have destroyed corn, wheat, and other crops. In the 1800s, clouds of Rocky Mountain locusts often flew eastward, eating food crops and other plants on the Great Plains. Even now, in the twenty-first century, locusts sometimes harm crops in Idaho and other western states. Locusts are also serious pests in Africa and India.

Desert locust

Cicadas are NOT locusts.

Cicadas are related to aphids, leafhoppers, and spittlebugs—all members of the insect order Homoptera. All of these insects have sucking mouthparts. To feed, they pierce a root or stem, then suck sap from the plant. Usually the plants are not harmed. Also, cicadas cannot bite or sting. They are harmless to people.

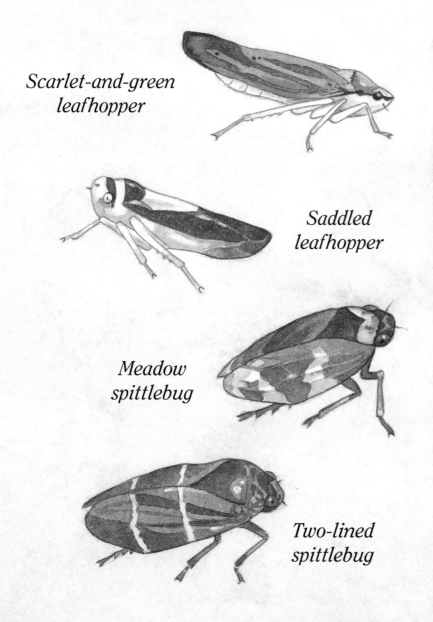

Scarlet-and-green leafhopper

Saddled leafhopper

Meadow spittlebug

Two-lined spittlebug

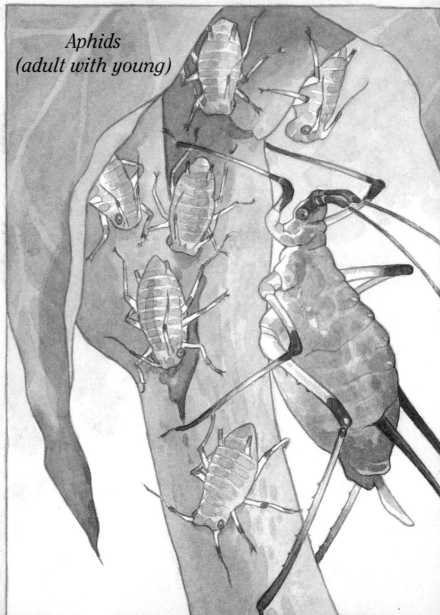

Aphids (adult with young)

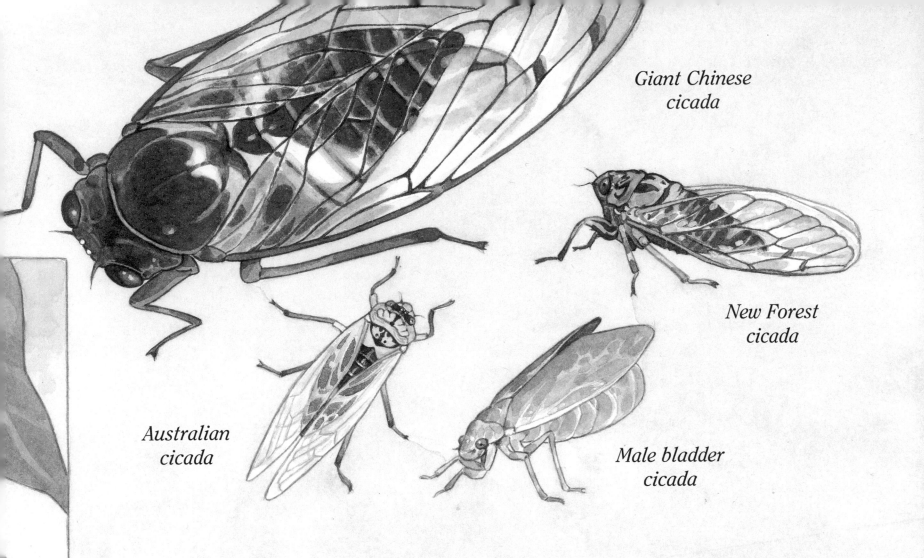

Giant Chinese
cicada

New Forest
cicada

Australian
cicada

Male bladder
cicada

More than 2,500 species of cicadas live on Earth, with new kinds still being discovered. Australia has several hundred species. Scientists expect to identify many more there. England has just one, the New Forest cicada, which may have died out.

Most cicadas measure about an inch or two long and are brown, black, or green in color. Some cicadas are big: a Chinese species is seven inches long, and its wing span is eight inches. Some are colorful: a species in Ecuador with red and green wing markings is called the stop-and-go cicada. Some are odd-looking: male bladder cicadas of Australia have large, balloon-like abdomens.

With their exceptionally long lives and huge numbers, the periodical cicadas of North America get plenty of attention. However, every year, smaller numbers of other kinds of cicadas emerge from the ground and fill summer days with their buzzing songs. They are often called dog-day cicadas. They are also called annual cicadas, since some emerge as adults every year.

Most adult annual, or dog-day, cicadas emerge in July and August, usually the hottest time in summer. Some people think the term *dog days* refers to dogs, and how they can suffer (without water and shade) in summertime.

Dog-day cicadas

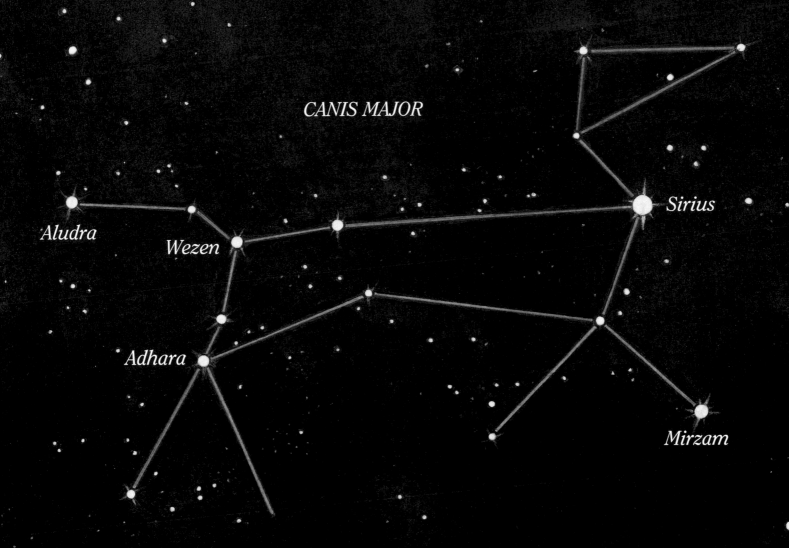

CANIS MAJOR

Aludra

Wezen

Adhara

Sirius

Mirzam

Dog days is actually a term used by ancient people who studied the night sky. They called one group of stars Canis Major—meaning the "big dog." In this constellation, the brightest star is Sirius, the Dog Star. In fact, Sirius is the brightest of all stars seen from Earth (except for our sun, which is also a star). In the summer, Sirius rises and sets with the sun. Ancient Egyptians and Romans believed that heat from Sirius the Dog Star was added to heat from the sun. So they called the warmest weeks of summer the "dog days."

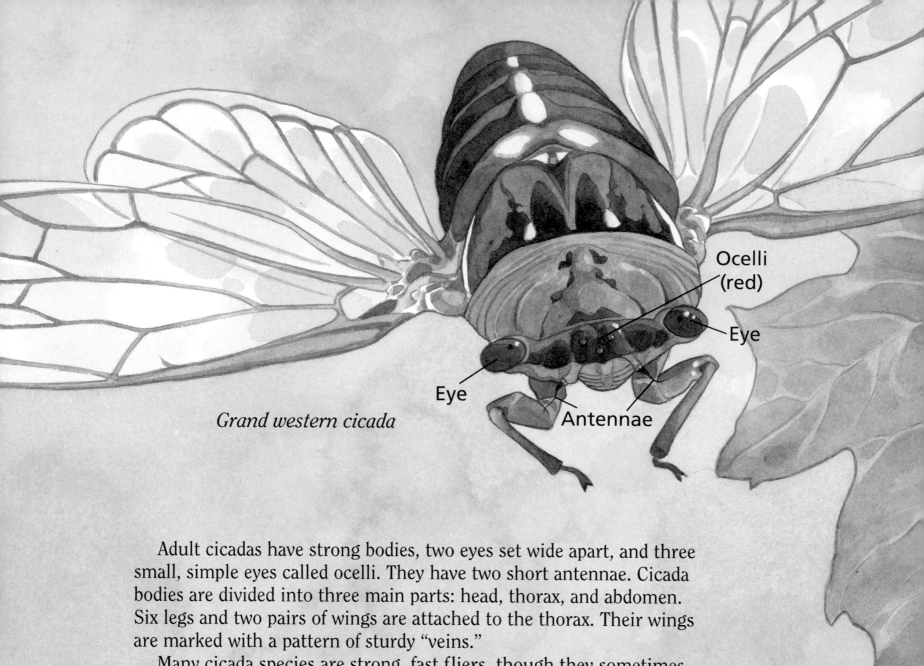

Ocelli
(red)

Eye

Eye

Antennae

Grand western cicada

Adult cicadas have strong bodies, two eyes set wide apart, and three small, simple eyes called ocelli. They have two short antennae. Cicada bodies are divided into three main parts: head, thorax, and abdomen. Six legs and two pairs of wings are attached to the thorax. Their wings are marked with a pattern of sturdy "veins."

Many cicada species are strong, fast fliers, though they sometimes smack into tree limbs or other objects. This doesn't seem to harm them; they have tough bodies. Cicadas grip tree bark with strong claws, then suck fluids from the plant. They do this mostly to take in water, to avoid drying out and to keep cool on hot summer days.

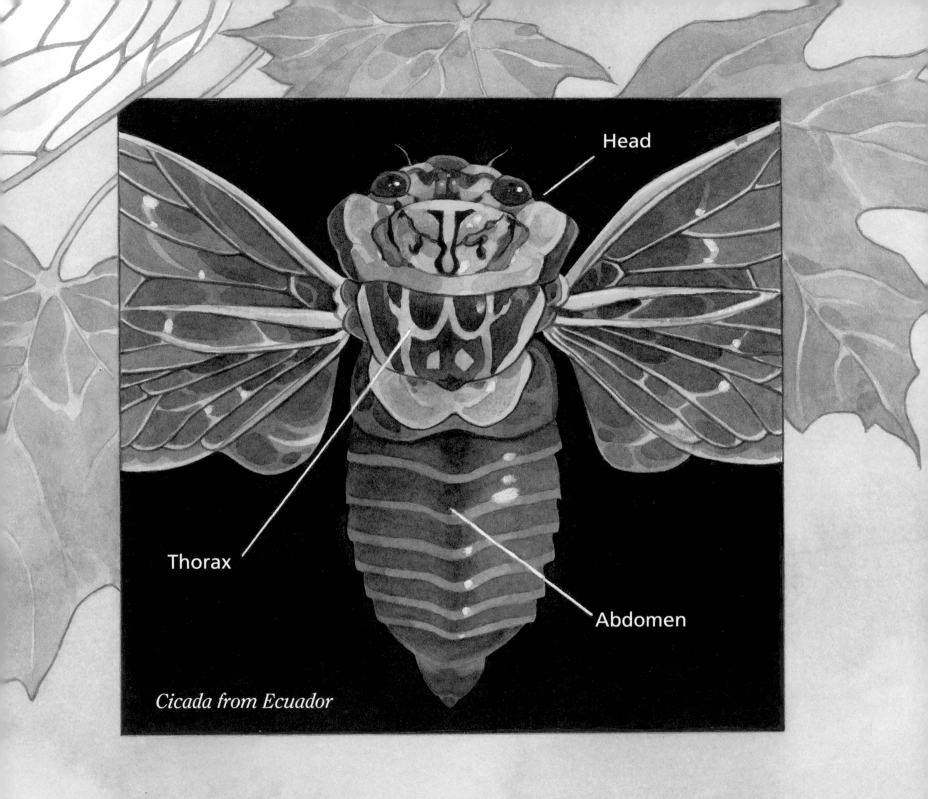

Head

Thorax

Abdomen

Cicada from Ecuador

To make a chirping sound,
a male cricket scrapes
part of one wing
against part of the other.

14

Just as male birds sing to attract females, male cicadas try to lure females with their songs. Cicada music is usually a loud buzzing or humming sound, but each cicada species has its own unique song that varies in tone and rhythm.

Many insects, including crickets and katydids, make sounds by rubbing body parts together. Cicadas do it in a different way. Each male cicada has two tymbals—thin membranes supported by strong ribs—located at the sides of its abdomen. When the cicada tightens muscles attached to its tymbals, they buckle inward and make a clicking sound. When the muscles relax, the tymbals snap back into position and make another click. This can be done more than three hundred times per second! The sound is amplified because a male cicada's abdomen is mostly hollow, like a drum.

Tymbal

CICADA LIFE CYCLE

Whether a cicada lives for one year, seven years, or seventeen years, its life span is made up of three stages: egg, nymph, and adult.

With its sharp-tipped ovipositor ("egg depositor"), a female cicada cuts slits in plants, often in tree twigs, and lays eggs there.

Tiny nymphs hatch from the eggs and drop to the ground.

With their strong front legs, nymphs burrow into the soil and begin to suck fluids from plant roots.

After their wings unfold and dry, the cicadas crawl or fly high in trees. The males start their buzzing music, the females respond, and the whole cicada life cycle starts again.

The nymphs climb a tree, post, or other standing object. Gripping it tightly, they undergo one more, final change. Their exoskeletons split down the back, and adult cicadas wriggle out.

Nymphs continue to feed and grow, changing their exoskeletons four times. Then, the cicada nymphs wait for the soil to warm—a signal that it is time to dig out.

A cicada nymph's hard skin is called its exoskeleton ("outer skeleton"). In order to grow, a nymph must break out of its old exoskeleton, emerging with a soft skin that soon hardens into its new, bigger exoskeleton. This process is called metamorphosis.

Like all cicadas, periodical cicadas have a three-stage life cycle: egg, nymph, and adult. However, they spend many, many years in the nymph stage. Then they suddenly appear—by the millions! It seems like magic, and so periodical cicada species were given the scientific name *Magicicada*.

These cicadas all emerge in a week or two, and often many of them appear in just one night. This is why there are news reports of a great insect "invasion." However, the cicadas do not swarm in from far away (like locusts). They emerge from underfoot—from the soil of lawns, backyards, parks, roadsides. For thirteen or seventeen years they have been neighbors, hidden underground. Then they emerge for their final, adult stage of life.

In the morning, people discover that the soil is pockmarked with countless small holes—the openings of tunnels from which the cicada nymphs emerged. Thousands of these holes can be found beneath a single big tree. By dawn, some cicada stragglers still come from the soil, crawl along the ground, or climb trees. Already, many adult cicadas have wriggled from their nymph "skins."

This final change takes about an hour. A newly emerged adult cicada is milky white. Its wings look like thick little flaps. The cicada pumps a fluid into the network of veins that support the wings. They expand to full size. Within two or three hours, the periodical cicada's body turns black. The wing veins turn bright orange, and the bulging eyes, bright red.

A few days after emerging from underground, male cicadas begin their buzzing sounds. Concentrating in trees, they are often close together in "chorusing centers" that attract females. The numbers of singing males can be huge—up to three-quarters of a million cicadas per acre. Their sound can be very loud—nearly as loud as the roar of a jet airplane's engine. (Fortunately, cicadas stop singing in the evening, so people living nearby can have quiet nights.)

Insect-eating birds flock in to feast on periodical cicadas, which are easier to catch than other cicada species. Grackles, starlings, jays, kestrels, crows, and other birds are attracted to the chorusing centers. Dogs, raccoons, and skunks catch cicadas on or near the ground. However, cicadas' numbers are so great that predators eat their fill, day after day, and there are still plenty of cicadas left alive to mate. Periodical cicadas are not good at avoiding predators, but overwhelm their enemies with sheer numbers.

Periodical cicadas are safe from one type of predator, however. Most kinds of cicadas in North America may face a special predator—the cicada killer. This big wasp does not sting people, but it is deadly to cicadas. First, female cicada killers dig burrows in the soil. The burrows can be several feet deep, with side branches.

Then each cicada killer hunts for cicadas, one at a time. She grips the insect with her long legs, then stings it. The cicada is alive but paralyzed. The wasp flies to its burrow, carrying its prey. Inside the burrow, the wasp lays an egg on the cicada's body. About two weeks later, a larva hatches from the egg. It feeds on the cicada, then spins a cocoon of mud and silk. A year later, in the next summer, adult cicada killers emerge from their cocoons and from their underground burrows. By then, adult periodical cicadas have all died, so the big wasps hunt other kinds of cicadas.

After mating, female periodical cicadas fly or crawl to the ends of tree branches. They cut slits in the twigs with the sharp end of their ovipositors. In each slit they lay between ten and thirty eggs, then move to another twig. A female can lay as many as six hundred eggs.

This egg-laying may cut off the flow of water and nutrients to the twig's end. Often the end of the branch and a few leaves die. Trees are not seriously harmed. The dead brown leaves that people see along roadsides and in backyards and parks are called "flagging"—and are a last dramatic reminder of the remarkable cicada spectacle that occurred weeks before. (By the time these "flags" appear, all adult cicadas are dead. At the most, they had five weeks of adult life.)

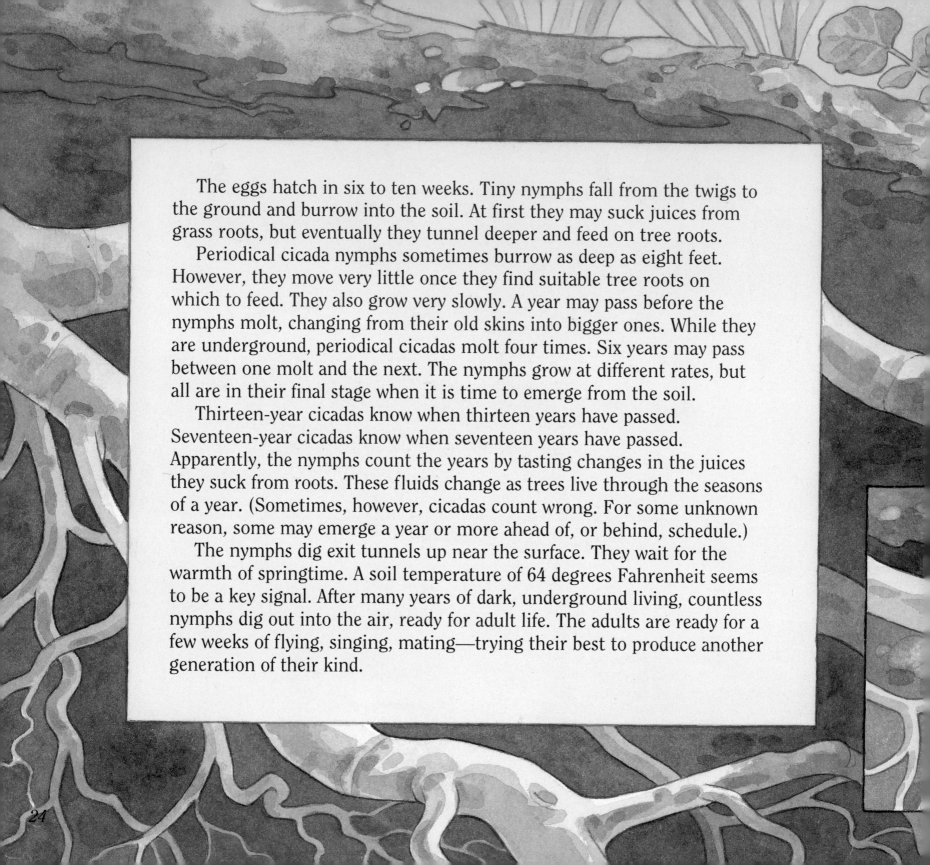

The eggs hatch in six to ten weeks. Tiny nymphs fall from the twigs to the ground and burrow into the soil. At first they may suck juices from grass roots, but eventually they tunnel deeper and feed on tree roots.

Periodical cicada nymphs sometimes burrow as deep as eight feet. However, they move very little once they find suitable tree roots on which to feed. They also grow very slowly. A year may pass before the nymphs molt, changing from their old skins into bigger ones. While they are underground, periodical cicadas molt four times. Six years may pass between one molt and the next. The nymphs grow at different rates, but all are in their final stage when it is time to emerge from the soil.

Thirteen-year cicadas know when thirteen years have passed. Seventeen-year cicadas know when seventeen years have passed. Apparently, the nymphs count the years by tasting changes in the juices they suck from roots. These fluids change as trees live through the seasons of a year. (Sometimes, however, cicadas count wrong. For some unknown reason, some may emerge a year or more ahead of, or behind, schedule.)

The nymphs dig exit tunnels up near the surface. They wait for the warmth of springtime. A soil temperature of 64 degrees Fahrenheit seems to be a key signal. After many years of dark, underground living, countless nymphs dig out into the air, ready for adult life. The adults are ready for a few weeks of flying, singing, mating—trying their best to produce another generation of their kind.

While laying eggs, female cicadas often choose the twigs of young trees growing in plentiful sunshine. Such trees are likely to thrive for many years. The periodical cicadas sipping on the trees' roots will also thrive.

Aboveground, a lot can happen in thirteen or seventeen years. If a tree dies, cicada nymphs can tunnel in search of living tree roots. However, if acres of forest are cut down and replaced with buildings and pavement, a whole population of cicadas can be wiped out. When the time for a mass emergence arrives, no cicadas appear from underground.

By cutting down forests and making other habitat changes, people have caused local cicada populations to disappear. Two entire broods have become extinct. One was Brood XI, which lived in the Connecticut River valley of Massachusetts and Connecticut. The other was Brood XXI, which lived in parts of the Florida panhandle and along the Mississippi–Alabama border.

People are worried about the future of the amazing periodical cicadas. They know that the key to cicada survival is protection of the forest habitats where they still live.

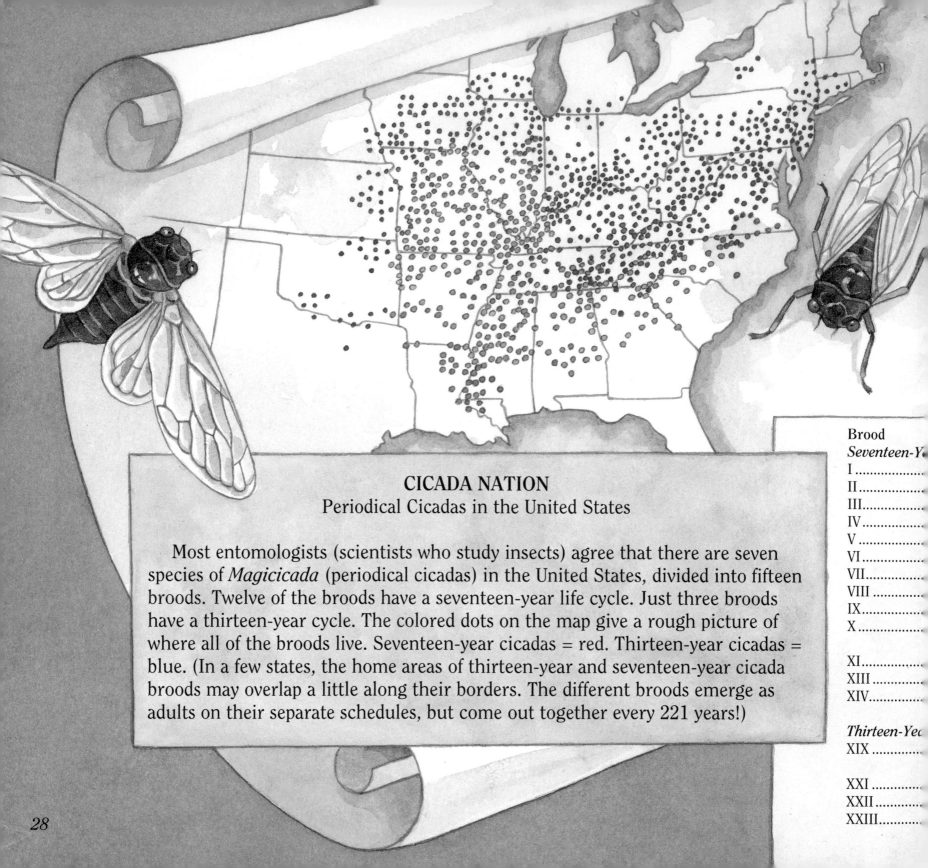

CICADA NATION
Periodical Cicadas in the United States

Most entomologists (scientists who study insects) agree that there are seven species of *Magicicada* (periodical cicadas) in the United States, divided into fifteen broods. Twelve of the broods have a seventeen-year life cycle. Just three broods have a thirteen-year cycle. The colored dots on the map give a rough picture of where all of the broods live. Seventeen-year cicadas = red. Thirteen-year cicadas = blue. (In a few states, the home areas of thirteen-year and seventeen-year cicada broods may overlap a little along their borders. The different broods emerge as adults on their separate schedules, but come out together every 221 years!)

Brood
Seventeen-Y
I.................
II.................
III.................
IV.................
V.................
VI.................
VII.................
VIII.................
IX.................
X.................

XI.................
XIII.................
XIV.................

Thirteen-Ye
XIX.................

XXI.................
XXII.................
XXIII.................

The ranges of the different broods vary a lot. Brood VII exists in parts of just two north-central counties of New York. Some other broods appear in a dozen or more states. The chart below lists the existing broods, the years in which they emerge, and where they live. (It includes two extinct broods.)

When news reports alert people to this spectacular event, some people are disappointed. They wonder, "Where are the cicadas? Why don't we see them?"

The answer is that cicadas appear only where they have always lived. Adult cicadas don't travel far. Generation after generation, they live in the same area. You can find them in one corner of a state or in and near a few towns—but not the entire state. Even within a community, the cicadas will emerge in one neighborhood, but not another. You may have to travel to see them.

Years of Emergence	Region
1978, 1995, 2012, 2029, etc.	Virginia, West Virginia
1979, 1996, 2013, 2030, etc.	Connecticut, Maryland, New Jersey, New York, North Carolina, Pennsylvania, Virginia
1980, 1997, 2014, 2031, etc.	Illinois, Iowa, Missouri
1981, 1998, 2015, 2032, etc.	Iowa, Kansas, Missouri, Nebraska, Oklahoma, Texas
1982, 1999, 2016, 2033, etc.	Maryland, Ohio, Pennsylvania, Virginia, West Virginia
1983, 2000, 2017, 2034, etc.	Georgia, North Carolina, South Carolina
1967, 1984, 2001, 2018, etc.	New York
1968, 1985, 2002, 2019, etc.	Ohio, Pennsylvania, West Virginia
1969, 1986, 2003, 2020, etc.	North Carolina, Virginia, West Virginia
1970, 1987, 2004, 2021, etc.	Delaware, Georgia, Illinois, Indiana, Kentucky, Maryland, Michigan, New Jersey, New York, North Carolina, Ohio, Pennsylvania, Tennessee, Virginia, West Virginia
Extinct (last hatch in 1954)	Connecticut, Massachusetts
1973, 1990, 2007, 2024, etc.	Illinois, Indiana, Iowa, Wisconsin
1974, 1991, 2008, 2025, etc.	Georgia, Indiana, Kentucky, Maryland, Massachusetts, New Jersey, New York, North Carolina, Ohio, Pennsylvania, Tennessee, Virginia, West Virginia
1972, 1985, 1998, 2011, etc.	Alabama, Arkansas, Georgia, Indiana, Illinois, Kentucky, Louisiana, Maryland, Mississippi, Missouri, North Carolina, Oklahoma, South Carolina, Tennessee, Virginia
Extinct (last hatch in 1870)	Alabama, Florida, Mississippi
1988, 2001, 2014, 2027, etc.	Louisiana, Mississippi
1989, 2002, 2015, 2028, etc.	Arkansas, Illinois, Indiana, Kentucky, Louisiana, Mississippi, Missouri, Tennessee

Cicadas are well-liked insects all over the world. In Asia, Africa, and Latin America, they are a source of food. (In general, over a thousand species of insects are human food in ninety nations.) In China, cicadas are cooked on skewers or stir-fried. There are other popular recipes. Some people say that cicadas taste like shrimp. Centuries ago, Native Americans looked forward to the years when periodical cicadas suddenly appeared. The loud buzzing chorus signaled a few weeks of abundant food.

Cicadas are also part of ancient folktales and sayings. In China, the phrase *to shed the golden cicada skin* means to fool enemies by using disguises or decoys. French people are especially fond of cicadas. Since 1895, the cicada, or *cigale*, has been the official symbol of Provence, in southern France. Gift shops sell all sorts of cigale-shaped products, such as jewelry, soaps, magnets, and salt and pepper shakers.

Kite

Cigales are symbols of summertime and happiness in Provence. They are also believed to bring good luck. Many homes in Provence have a ceramic cicada hung by the entrance door.

When periodical cicadas suddenly appear in the United States, not everyone is pleased. Some people fear insects and are upset about cicadas surrounding their homes. The noisy buzzing is a nuisance. Some would say it is an ordeal! Living in the midst of a *Magicicada* emergence can be a challenge.

It can also be an honor—to live in an area where one of nature's great spectacles takes place. It can be awe-inspiring—to know how long these cicadas have waited for their few weeks of adult life, finally out in the air and sunshine.

It can be a time to celebrate. "Hurray! The cicadas are here!"

Jade cicada

Author's Note: A Life with Cicadas

Every summer during my childhood in western New York, dog-day cicadas buzzed from high in the trees. And every summer, my brother and I searched tree trunks for their dry, hollow nymph bodies. We competed: who could find the most of these strange-looking "husks"?

Much later, as a nature photographer, I was able to take a closeup picture of a cicada that had just emerged from its nymph skin. This was not in some wild place. The cicada nymph had climbed the stem of a tomato plant in a New Jersey garden.

The summer of 1979 brought an extraordinary event to New York's Hudson River valley, where I now live: the emergence of Brood II of seventeen-year cicadas. In parts of Nyack, New York, I found these red-eyed insects everywhere—crawling over the ground and sidewalks, climbing trees and fence posts. Thousands of male cicadas filled the late June days with their loud buzzing.

I took some photos, but the great spectacle was soon over. Sadly, I added the number 17 to 1979 and vowed to be ready for the next generation, in 1996. In that year, I visited Nyack many times, witnessing another mass emergence of Brood II. I wanted to get a new colony started near my home and followed the advice of an entomologist. She suggested that I collect twigs where female cicadas had laid their eggs. With hand clippers I pruned a few trees of these twigs, then scattered them in a protected forest near my home.

As I write these words, nymphs that emerged from those twigs are underground in the woods, well along in their seventeen-year lives. Seventeen years added to 1996 equals 2013. That year, I hope to see if my efforts to transplant cicadas worked. Most important, I simply hope to once again celebrate the amazing lives of seventeen-year cicadas.

Sources and More Information About Cicadas

The best Web site for cicada information is Cicada Mania (www.cicadamania.com*). It reports on the emergence of different broods of periodical cicadas. It also includes information about all cicada species, features cicada photographs and news stories, and has links to other good cicada sites and sources of cicada research at several universities.

Information sources for this book include university science Web sites (see cicadamania.com). Some helpful books and articles are:

Barron, James. "Cicadas: They're Back." *New York Times*, June 4, 1996, pp. C1, C9.

Kritsky, Gene. *In Ohio's Backyards: Periodical Cicadas*. Columbus, OH: Ohio Biological Survey, 1994.

Kritsky, Gene. *Periodical Cicadas: The Plague and the Puzzle*. Indianapolis: Indiana Academy of Science, 2004.

Marchand, Peter. "Jamming Cicadas." *Natural History*, June, 2002, pp. 36–39.

Nickens, T. Edward. "Insect Opera." *Audubon*, May–June 2000, pp. 25–30.

*Active at time of publication